HOW TO OPEN A
COMPUTER STORE

A Comprehensive Guide to Starting, Running and Growing Your Own Tech Retail Business

MORRIS WILLIS

TABLE OF CONTENTS

Introduction

Starting a successful computer store requires a comprehensive understanding of this ever-evolving landscape. This guide is meticulously designed to support aspiring entrepreneurs diving into the vibrant world of computer retail. It serves as your ultimate companion, offering navigation through the intricate process of initiating, operating, and thriving within the computer retail industry.

Inside these pages, you'll discover a reservoir of invaluable insights, cultivated from years of collective experience within the computer retail domain. From decoding the nuances of the computer market to devising an impactful business strategy, procuring the right inventory, nurturing customer relationships, and harnessing the latest technological advancements, this guide covers every facet.

Building a thriving computer store goes beyond mere establishment; it's about creating a haven for tech enthusiasts, a trusted resource for professionals, and an integral part of the community. It revolves around curating an extensive inventory, providing expert guidance, and seamlessly integrating into the community's growth.

Our goal with this guide is to ignite your passion, crystalize your vision, and equip you with the essential tools and knowledge needed to construct a thriving computer store. Whether you're a seasoned industry veteran or stepping into the world of computer retail for the first time, this book is poised to be your unwavering companion, a wise mentor, and a guiding light as you embark on this exhilarating journey of establishing your computer store.

Why Start a Computer Store?

Starting a computer store presents an enticing array of reasons that make it a compelling venture. Firstly, these stores serve as vital hubs within communities, offering an extensive range of technological tools, components, and expertise crucial for enthusiasts, professionals, and everyday users. By establishing a computer store, one steps into a role beyond entrepreneurship; it becomes a pillar of support, catering to indispensable needs and fostering trust among customers.

The market for computer-related products and services exhibits a consistent and evergreen demand. Regardless of economic fluctuations, there's a perpetual need for gadgets, accessories, repairs, and technological know-how, ensuring a steady customer base—a significant advantage for aspiring business owners seeking stability in their endeavors.

The versatility within the computer retail industry stands out as another compelling aspect. Whether one's interest lies in gaming gear, hardware, software, or specialized solutions, there exists ample room to carve out a niche. This flexibility allows entrepreneurs to align their store with their passions, ensuring not just financial viability but also personal fulfillment in catering to a specific audience.

Beyond retail transactions, computer stores can foster strong community ties. A well-managed store can transcend its role by organizing workshops, training sessions, and tech events, serving as a knowledge hub that brings people together. This active engagement not only enhances the store's reputation but also cultivates lasting relationships with customers, fostering loyalty and trust.

Ultimately, starting a computer store offers the canvas for an entrepreneurial journey filled with innovation and personalized service. Entrepreneurs have the opportunity to curate a unique retail experience, offering not just products but expertise, exceptional service, and an inviting environment that distinguishes their store from larger, impersonal chains.

In essence, the decision to start a computer store transcends mere business; it's about becoming an integral part of a community, meeting essential needs, sharing expertise, and leaving a lasting impression while embracing the rewards and challenges of entrepreneurship.

Is a Computer Store Right for You?

Determining if a computer store is the right venture for you involves a thoughtful consideration of various factors that align with your interests, skills, and entrepreneurial goals. Firstly, a passion for technology and a deep understanding of computer hardware, software, and peripherals can be a pivotal starting point. If you find yourself constantly immersed in the world of computers, troubleshooting technical issues, or staying updated with the latest trends, a computer store might be a natural fit for your expertise.

A keen interest in customer service is paramount. Running a successful computer store involves not just selling products but also providing technical support, guidance, and solutions to customers with diverse needs and proficiency levels. Your ability to communicate effectively, patiently address concerns, and offer tailored recommendations can significantly impact customer satisfaction and loyalty.

Financial considerations play a crucial role as well. Assessing the initial investment required to set up a computer store, including inventory, store setup, equipment, and operational costs, is essential. Additionally, understanding the potential revenue streams, profit margins, and the competitive landscape within the computer retail industry can help gauge the financial viability of such a venture.

Flexibility and adaptability are key traits for success in this dynamic field. The technology landscape evolves rapidly, requiring store owners to stay abreast of emerging trends, new products, and changing consumer preferences. Being open to diversifying product offerings, embracing innovative marketing strategies, and adapting to technological advancements is integral to staying competitive in the market.

Lastly, the commitment to continuous learning and improvement is fundamental. The computer industry is characterized by constant innovation and change. A willingness to learn, upgrade skills, and evolve with the industry is crucial for sustained success.

Determining if a computer store is the right fit involves a blend of technical expertise, customer-centric approach, financial preparedness, adaptability to change, and a commitment to ongoing learning. Evaluating these aspects against your personal interests and entrepreneurial aspirations can help determine if pursuing a computer store aligns with your vision and capabilities.

Chapter 1:
The Computer Store Industry

The computer store industry stands as an integral part of local communities, providing indispensable tools, expertise, and materials for computer repairs, upgrades, and tech-related projects. This diverse sector encompasses a wide range of establishments, from small shops to expansive chain retailers. At its core, the industry is dedicated to meeting the needs of homeowners, tech enthusiasts and professionals.

Central to the computer store industry is its comprehensive offering of products and services. These stores stock an extensive array of computer components, peripherals, software, accessories, and gadgets, serving as go-to destinations for all things tech-related.

Adaptability is key to the success of computer stores. They continuously evolve to align with customer preferences and industry advancements. Whether it's embracing eco-friendly products, introducing cutting-edge technology, or leveraging digital platforms for customer interaction, these stores stay ahead by catering to changing trends and demands.

A hallmark of computer stores is their commitment to personalized service and expert advice. Customers rely on these stores for guidance on product selection, troubleshooting, and tailored recommendations. Staffed by knowledgeable professionals well-versed in the latest tech trends, these stores offer invaluable assistance to customers.

Again, beyond commerce, computer stores often serve as community hubs, fostering connections and camaraderie among locals. They organize events, workshops, and educational programs, contributing to the social fabric of neighborhoods and creating spaces for learning and interaction.

Despite the emergence of online retail and large-scale tech outlets, computer stores retain their relevance by offering personalized service, convenience, and a local touch. They embody trust, reliability, and accessibility, catering to customers seeking expertise and a sense of community in their tech shopping experiences. As the industry continues to evolve, these stores remain vital resources, empowering individuals to bring their tech projects and aspirations to life, one component or device at a time.

Trends and Opportunities

Understanding the computer market involves delving into its multifaceted landscape, influenced by technological advancements, consumer behavior, and industry trends. At its core, this market encompasses a vast array of products, services, and segments, catering to diverse consumer needs and preferences.

One pivotal aspect of comprehending the computer market is acknowledging its dynamic nature. Technological innovation drives rapid changes, influencing the demand for various devices, software, and accessories. From laptops, desktops, and tablets to peripherals like keyboards, mice, and monitors, the market is expansive and ever-evolving. Understanding these technological shifts is crucial for businesses aiming to stay competitive and relevant.

Moreover, consumer behavior plays a significant role in shaping the computer market. The preferences, buying habits, and expectations of customers continually evolve. Factors like convenience, performance, design, and price sensitivity impact purchasing decisions. Recognizing these patterns helps businesses tailor their offerings to meet consumer demands effectively.

Segmentation within the computer market further adds complexity. It comprises different categories such as gaming computers, business-oriented devices, educational tech, and specialized equipment for creative professionals. Each segment carries its unique characteristics and requirements, requiring businesses to target their products and services accordingly.

Furthermore, the influence of online retail and e-commerce cannot be overlooked. The shift towards digital platforms for purchasing computer-related products has reshaped the market dynamics. Accessibility, competitive pricing, and a wide array of choices offered by online retailers have altered how consumers interact with the market, impacting traditional brick-and-mortar stores.

Lastly, staying updated with industry trends, emerging technologies, and market forecasts is essential for businesses seeking longevity and growth in the computer market. Whether it's the rise of artificial intelligence, the integration of IoT (Internet of Things), or the demand for sustainable tech solutions, being aware of these trends allows businesses to anticipate shifts and adapt their strategies accordingly.

In essence, understanding the computer market requires a holistic approach that considers technological advancements, consumer behaviors, segmentation, online influences, and industry trends. By comprehending these factors, businesses can navigate this dynamic market landscape more effectively, making informed decisions to meet the evolving needs of tech-savvy consumers.

What Sets a Computer Store Apart

A computer store distinguishes itself through various factors that set it apart in the retail landscape. These aspects not only define its uniqueness but also contribute significantly to its success and customer appeal.

Firstly, a computer store stands out due to its specialized expertise and tailored service. Unlike general retail outlets, computer stores are staffed with knowledgeable professionals who possess a deep understanding of technology. Customers benefit from personalized guidance and advice on a wide range of tech-related queries, from choosing the right components to troubleshooting issues. This expertise creates a sense of trust and reliability, fostering a loyal customer base seeking specialized assistance.

Secondly, the product range offered by a computer store sets it apart. These stores curate a comprehensive selection of computer hardware, software, peripherals, and accessories, catering to both casual users and tech enthusiasts. The diversity and depth of their inventory ensure that customers can find niche products and the latest innovations under one roof, making the shopping experience convenient and comprehensive. Moreover, the emphasis on customer service distinguishes computer stores. Beyond selling products, these establishments prioritize providing exceptional service. They offer repair and maintenance services, product demonstrations, and after-sales support. This commitment to customer satisfaction fosters long-term relationships and encourages repeat business.

Another aspect that sets a computer store apart is its community engagement. Many of these stores actively engage with their local communities through workshops, seminars, and tech-related events. By providing educational resources and being a hub for tech enthusiasts to gather and share knowledge, these stores become integral parts of their neighborhoods, fostering a sense of camaraderie and learning.

Additionally, the adaptability and agility of computer stores in keeping up with industry trends contribute to their uniqueness. These stores are quick to embrace emerging technologies, sustainability initiatives, and advancements in the digital space. By staying abreast of the ever-evolving tech landscape, they remain relevant and attractive to customers seeking the latest innovations and solutions.

In essence, what sets a computer store apart is its blend of expertise, diverse product offerings, exceptional customer service, community engagement, and adaptability. Collectively, these elements create a distinct identity for the store, making it a go-to destination for customers seeking not just products but a holistic and fulfilling tech shopping experience.

Passion and Vision

Passion and vision serve as the driving force behind the inception and growth of a thriving computer store. The fervor for technology and innovation ignites a dedication to offering a wide array of quality products and exceptional service, catering to tech enthusiasts, businesses, and everyday users alike.

Vision, within the context of a computer store, involves a comprehensive blueprint delineating the store's objectives, target audience, and services. It's about envisioning the computer store as more than just a retail space; it's a knowledge hub, offering expert advice and an extensive range of cutting-edge products. This vision encompasses the store's pivotal role in providing solutions, fostering strong customer relationships, and establishing itself as a trusted authority in the realm of technology solutions and support.

The fusion of passion and vision brings vibrancy to the store's ethos. It fuels an unwavering commitment to top-notch products, expert guidance, and unparalleled customer service. This drive enables the store to cater not only to tech needs but also to offer expertise and a warm, welcoming atmosphere where customers feel valued and understood.

Furthermore, this union of passion and vision attracts like-minded individuals—passionate employees who share the same zeal for serving customers and making meaningful contributions to the tech community. It fosters a culture of collaboration and a shared dedication to the store's mission, promoting an environment of excellence and innovation.

Ultimately, in embarking on the journey of establishing a computer store, passion fuels the excitement, while vision provides the strategic direction and sense of purpose required to create a store that stands out as an indispensable resource within the tech community.

Chapter 2:
Market Research and Planning

In the world of business, the phrase "knowledge is power" couldn't be more accurate. Before embarking on the journey of starting your own computer store, you need to arm yourself with a deep understanding of your market and a well-thought-out plan. This chapter is all about laying the groundwork for your computer store venture, and it starts with four key components: Understanding Your Target Market, Choosing the Right Location, Competitive Analysis, and Creating a Business Plan.

Understanding Your Target Market

Understanding your target market is pivotal when establishing and operating a computer store. To begin, conducting extensive market research is crucial for pinpointing the specific needs, preferences, and behaviors of potential customers. This involves analyzing demographics like age, income, location, and lifestyle to craft a comprehensive profile of your target audience. It's vital to grasp the unique requirements of your local community. Consider elements such as prevalent project types, common repair needs, and any specific trends or preferences in the area. This understanding empowers you to tailor your inventory, services, and marketing strategies to meet the demands of your specific market.

Assessing the competition is equally important. Studying nearby computer stores helps identify gaps in their offerings or areas where your store can stand out. Understanding competitors' strengths and weaknesses aids in shaping your distinct value proposition and establishing your position within the market. Additionally, engaging directly with potential customers through surveys, focus groups, or community events offers invaluable insights. Listening to their feedback, understanding their challenges, and gauging their preferences helps refine your product selection, pricing strategies, and customer service efforts to better fulfill their needs.

A profound understanding of your target market lays the groundwork for a computer store that resonates with and caters to your customers' demands. It allows you to customize your offerings, create an engaging shopping experience, and cultivate enduring relationships within your community, all of which contribute to the success of your business.

Choosing the Right Location

Once you've thoroughly understood your computer store's intended audience, the next pivotal step is finding the perfect spot to set up shop. The location is absolutely critical, and here's why it holds such immense importance:

Visibility and Accessibility: Your store needs to be easily seen and accessible to your potential customers. Optimal locations typically boast high pedestrian traffic and proximity to residential areas, ensuring convenient access for shoppers.

Assessing Competition: Knowing the existing competition in your chosen area is crucial. Are there established computer stores nearby? What makes your store unique? Identifying gaps in the market or catering to underserved customer segments can give your store a competitive edge.

Matching Demographics: Ensure your chosen location aligns with the demographics and preferences of your target market.

Zoning and Regulations: Local regulations and permits are key considerations. These guidelines can affect your store's layout, operating hours, and the range of products you can offer. Adhering to local laws is vital for a successful business.

Financial Evaluation: Conduct a thorough financial analysis of your potential location, considering factors like rent, utilities, and maintenance costs. Will this spot generate a favorable return on investment? Careful cost evaluation is crucial.

Consider teaming up with a commercial real estate agent who specializes in retail spaces. These professionals can assist in pinpointing locations that match your objectives, negotiate lease terms, and ensure your chosen spot becomes an asset rather than a liability.

Selecting the right location for your computer store lays the foundation for its success. A well-chosen spot can drive foot traffic, set you apart from competitors, and establish strong connections with your customer base. By contemplating these factors and seeking expert advice, you can make an informed decision that positions your store for success in the competitive retail landscape.

Competitive Analysis

Understanding the competitive landscape is pivotal in establishing a niche for your computer store within the market. A comprehensive analysis acts as your guiding compass, steering you through the intricate terrain of this industry by identifying strengths, weaknesses, opportunities, and threats. Here's a step-by-step approach:

Commence by compiling an exhaustive list of all existing computer stores in your selected area. However, broaden your scope beyond direct competitors. Consider nearby convenience stores, supermarkets, and even online computer outlets that might impact your market share. A broader perspective enriches your analysis.

For each competitor on your list, conduct a SWOT analysis. Identify their Strengths, like unique product offerings, robust brand recognition, or a loyal customer base. Acknowledge their Weaknesses, which might encompass inadequate customer service, limited product diversity, or outdated technology. Explore potential Opportunities they might be overlooking, such as untapped market segments or emerging consumer trends. Lastly, assess the Threats they face, such as new entrants, economic fluctuations, or shifts in consumer preferences. This analysis unveils invaluable insights into the competitive landscape.

Now, carve out your computer store's Unique Selling Proposition. What distinguishes your establishment? Your USP might be a commitment to offering locally sourced products, an unwavering dedication to exceptional customer service, or unique in-store experiences. Your USP serves as the magnet drawing customers to your store.

Dive into your competitors' pricing strategies. Do they target high-end consumers as premium stores or cater to budget-conscious shoppers? Some may strike a balance between these extremes. Align your pricing strategy with your target market and identified USP. Balancing competitiveness and profitability is key.

When possible, gather market share data for your chosen area. This data unveils insights into existing players' dominance. Understanding who holds the largest market share and where there might be underserved segments informs your strategic decisions.

Conducting a thorough competitive analysis is akin to mapping out your computer store's success route. It not only delineates your market's landscape but also spotlights growth opportunities and areas where your store can excel. By carefully assessing competitors' strengths, weaknesses, opportunities, and threats, refine your business concept, devise a winning strategy, and position your computer store for sustained success in a fiercely competitive market.

Crafting a Comprehensive Business Plan

Now that you've gained a profound understanding of your target market, selected an optimal location, and gleaned insights into your competition, it's time to synthesize all this valuable information into a structured business plan. A business plan is your blueprint for steering your computer store toward success. It encompasses several key components, each contributing to the overall framework of your vision:

Executive Summary: At the forefront of your business plan is the executive summary. This concise section encapsulates your business's essence, featuring your mission statement, overarching goals, and a summary of your financial forecasts.

Company Description: Dive deep into the intricacies of your computer store in the company description section. Paint a vivid picture of your venture, elucidating your vision, the array of products you intend to offer, your unique selling propositions, and the profile of your target market.

Market Analysis: Summarize the insights gleaned from your thorough market research. Include pertinent details about your target market's demographics, the strategic choice of your location, and the competitive landscape you've uncovered.

Organization and Management: Provide an organizational blueprint. Who comprises your key team members, and what roles will they fulfill? Highlight relevant experience and qualifications that bolster your team's ability to execute your business strategy.

Products and Services: Outline an exhaustive list of the products and services that your computer store will provide. Elaborate on any distinctive or specialty items in your inventory and elucidate your sourcing strategy.

Sales and Marketing: Articulate your sales and marketing strategies in detail. How will you entice and retain customers? Detail your advertising campaigns, promotional tactics, and the channels you'll employ to reach your audience effectively.

Funding Request: If you're seeking external financing, elucidate your funding needs. Specify precisely how you intend to allocate these funds and outline the terms you're seeking from potential investors or lenders.

Financial Projections: Underpin your plan with meticulous financial projections. Include comprehensive income statements, balance sheets, and cash flow statements that extend at least three to five years into the future. These projections offer a tangible picture of your financial trajectory.

Appendix: Finally, compile any supplemental documents that buttress your business plan. This might encompass market research data, resumes showcasing the expertise of key team members, and essential supplier agreements.

Remember that your business plan isn't a static document; it should evolve alongside your business. It serves as a dynamic tool for strategizing, decision-making, and effectively conveying your vision to potential investors and stakeholders. With a robust business plan in hand, you'll be better equipped to navigate the dynamic computer store landscape and steer your venture toward long-term success.

Chapter 3:
Legal and Regulatory Considerations

Starting and operating a computer store involves navigating a complex web of legal and regulatory requirements. Understanding and complying with these rules is essential to ensure the smooth and legal operation of your business. In this chapter, we'll explore the key legal and regulatory considerations for your computer store, including choosing the right business structure, obtaining permits and licenses, adhering to health and safety regulations, and managing taxation.

Choosing a Business Structure

One of the first decisions you'll need to make when starting your computer store is choosing the right business structure. The structure you select will have implications for your personal liability, taxation, and how you can raise capital. Here are some common business structures to consider:

Sole Proprietorship: This is the simplest and most common form of business ownership. As a sole proprietor, you have complete control over your computer store, but you are personally responsible for all business debts and liabilities. Your business income and expenses are reported on your personal tax return.

Partnership: If you plan to start your computer store with one or more partners, a partnership structure may be suitable. Partnerships can be general partnerships (where partners share equally in profits and liabilities) or limited partnerships (where some partners have limited liability). Like sole proprietors, partners report their share of business income and expenses on their personal tax returns.

Limited Liability Company (LLC): An LLC provides a level of personal liability protection for its owners (called members). Members are typically not personally responsible for the company's debts and liabilities. LLCs offer flexibility in management and taxation, as they can be taxed as a sole proprietorship, partnership, or corporation.

Corporation: A corporation is a separate legal entity from its owners (shareholders). This structure offers the most significant personal liability protection, as shareholders are generally not personally liable for the company's debts. Corporations also have the advantage of attracting outside investors by issuing shares of stock. However, corporations have more complex tax and regulatory requirements.

Cooperative (Co-op): A cooperative is owned and operated by its members, who share in the decision-making and profits. Computer store cooperatives are often formed by a group of individuals with a shared interest. Co-ops have unique governance structures and may be organized as LLCs, corporations, or other legal entities.

Choosing the right business structure is a critical decision that should align with your long-term goals and financial considerations. Consult with legal and financial advisors to assess the best option for your computer store.

Permits and Licenses

Running a computer store requires various permits and licenses to comply with local, state, and federal regulations. These licenses and permits demonstrate that your store meets specific health, safety, and operational standards. Here's an overview of the essential permits and licenses you may need:

Business License: Most cities or municipalities require businesses to obtain a general business license. This license allows you to operate legally within a specific jurisdiction. The requirements and fees for business licenses vary by location.

Sales Tax Permit: Also known as a sales tax license or resale permit, this allows your computer store to collect sales tax from customers on behalf of the state. It's necessary for selling taxable goods and services.

Building Permits: If you're constructing or renovating your store space, building permits are essential. They ensure that your construction plans comply with local building codes, safety standards, and zoning regulations.

Signage Permits: These permits are needed for any external signage you plan to install for your store. Regulations regarding size, placement, and type of signage vary by location and must be adhered to.

Occupational Permits: Depending on your locality, you might need specific occupational permits or licenses related to the computer retail industry. These could include licenses for handling hazardous materials, operating power tools, or providing certain services.

Health and Safety Permits: If your store offers services like key cutting or tool repair, you might need health and safety permits to ensure compliance with regulations related to these services.

It's essential to research and understand the specific permits and licenses required in your area. Contact your local government offices or regulatory authorities to obtain detailed information about the necessary permits and the application process. Non-compliance with these regulations can result in fines, legal issues, or even the closure of your business. Therefore, ensuring that you have all the required permits and licenses in place before opening your computer store is crucial for its legal and operational integrity.

Taxation

Understanding the taxation aspects of your computer store is crucial for managing your finances and complying with tax laws. Here are key tax considerations:

Sales Tax: Most states and local jurisdictions impose sales tax on the sale of tangible goods. You are responsible for collecting and remitting sales tax to the appropriate taxing authorities. It's essential to understand the specific tax rates and exemptions that apply to computer items in your area.

Income Tax: Your computer store's income is subject to federal and state income taxes. The business structure you choose will determine how your income is taxed. Sole proprietors report business income on their personal tax returns, while corporations have separate tax obligations.

Employee Payroll Taxes: If you have employees, you must withhold and remit payroll taxes, including federal income tax, Social Security tax, and Medicare tax. Employers also pay a portion of these taxes.

Property Tax: Real property, such as the land and buildings housing your computer store, is subject to property tax. The amount of property tax you pay depends on the assessed value of your property and local tax rates.

Licensing and Permit Fees: Some licenses and permits may have associated fees that must be paid on a regular basis.

Use Tax: If your state imposes a use tax, you may be required to pay it on items purchased out of state for use in your business.

Business Deductions: Take advantage of tax deductions available to computer stores. These may include deductions for business expenses such as rent, utilities, advertising, and employee salaries.

Accounting and Recordkeeping: Maintain accurate financial records and accounting practices to facilitate tax compliance and reporting. Consider working with a certified public accountant (CPA) or tax professional to ensure accuracy.

Tax Credits and Incentives: Research if there are any tax credits or incentives available for computer stores in your region. Some areas offer incentives for businesses that promote healthy eating or invest in energy-efficient equipment.

Filing Deadlines: Familiarize yourself with tax filing deadlines and make sure you submit all required tax forms and payments on time to avoid penalties and interest.

Navigating the complexities of taxation can be challenging, so it's advisable to consult with a tax professional or CPA with experience in the retail and computer industry. They can help you maximize deductions, plan for tax liabilities, and ensure compliance with tax laws.

The legal and regulatory considerations for a computer store are multifaceted and demand meticulous attention. Choosing the right business structure, obtaining the necessary permits and licenses, adhering to health and safety regulations, and managing taxation are fundamental aspects of running a successful and legally compliant computer store. By investing the time and effort to understand and meet these requirements, you lay a solid foundation for the growth and longevity of your business.

Chapter 4:
Financing Your Computer Store

Financing is a critical aspect of launching and sustaining a successful computer store. In this chapter, we will explore the key elements of financing your computer store, including estimating startup costs, securing funding from various sources, and managing your finances effectively.

Estimating Startup Costs

Before launching your computer store, it's vital to gauge the initial investment needed to kickstart your business. Accurately estimating startup expenses is key to securing funding and steering clear of financial hurdles. Consider these core components when calculating your startup costs:

Location Expenses: Cover costs for securing and preparing your store location, encompassing lease or purchase fees, renovations, and essential permits.

Equipment and Fixtures: Include expenses for purchasing or leasing vital equipment like display units, cash registers, shelving, and point-of-sale (POS) systems.

Inventory: Factor in the initial stock of computer products based on your store's size and focus.

Licenses and Permits: Account for fees tied to acquiring necessary licenses like health permits, business licenses, and signage permits.

Legal and Professional Fees: Budget for legal aid in structuring your business and reviewing contracts, as well as consultancy or advisory fees.

Marketing and Advertising: Allocate funds for marketing strategies and advertising campaigns to publicize your store's launch and draw in customers.

Employee Expenses: Set aside a budget for hiring, training, salaries, benefits, and recruitment expenses during the startup phase.

Utilities and Rent: Project monthly rent or lease payments, utility bills, and security deposits.

Insurance: Account for business insurance costs, including liability, property, and workers' compensation coverage.

Technology and Software: Budget for computer systems, software, and POS systems to manage sales and inventory.

Working Capital: Reserve funds for initial operational expenses, covering additional inventory, payroll, and cash flow until the store turns profitable.

Contingency Fund: Have a buffer for unexpected expenses or setbacks during the startup phase.

Marketing and Grand Opening: Allocate a budget for promotional events and marketing efforts for your store's grand opening.

Miscellaneous Expenses: Allow for various costs such as office supplies, signage, and initial marketing materials.

Develop a detailed financial plan encompassing these costs, providing a realistic estimate for your startup. Expect to review and adjust your budget as you refine your business plan and gather more information. This comprehensive approach will help set a strong financial foundation for your computer store's successful launch.

Securing Funding

Once you have a clear understanding of your startup costs, the next step is to secure the necessary funding. Financing your computer store may require a combination of personal savings, loans, investments, and grants. Here are some common sources of funding:

Personal Savings: Using your own savings to finance your computer store is a common and straightforward approach. It allows you to maintain full control of your business and eliminates the need to pay interest on loans.

Family and Friends: Some entrepreneurs turn to family members or close friends for financial support. While this can be an accessible source of funding, it's crucial to formalize any agreements in writing to avoid misunderstandings.

Small Business Loans: Banks and credit unions offer various types of small business loans, including term loans, lines of credit, and equipment financing. These loans often require a solid business plan and collateral.

SBA Loans: The U.S. Small Business Administration (SBA) provides loan programs to support small businesses. SBA loans typically have favorable terms and lower interest rates, but they also involve a rigorous application process.

Investors: Seek investors who are willing to provide capital in exchange for equity or a share of the profits. Angel investors, venture capitalists, and private equity firms are potential sources of investment.

Crowdfunding: Crowdfunding platforms, such as Kickstarter and Indiegogo, allow you to raise funds from a large number of people online. This method is particularly effective if you have a unique and compelling business concept.

Grants: Some government agencies, non-profit organizations, and foundations offer grants to support small businesses, especially those focused on community development or sustainable practices.

Supplier Financing: Negotiate favorable payment terms with your suppliers. Some suppliers may offer extended payment periods, allowing you to manage cash flow more effectively.

Franchise Opportunities: If you're considering opening a franchise computer store, the franchisor may provide financing options or assistance with securing loans.

Online Lenders: Online lending platforms offer various financing options, including short-term loans, business lines of credit, and invoice financing. These options may be more accessible for newer businesses.

Government Programs: Research local and state government programs that provide financial assistance, grants, or tax incentives to small businesses, especially those creating jobs or contributing to the local economy.

Alternative Funding: Explore alternative funding sources, such as merchant cash advances, factoring, or peer-to-peer lending. These options may be suitable for businesses with unique financing needs.

To secure funding successfully, you'll need to prepare a compelling business plan that demonstrates the viability and profitability of your computer store. Lenders and investors want to see that you have a clear vision, a solid market strategy, and a realistic financial forecast. Be prepared to provide financial statements, cash flow projections, and any collateral if required.

Managing Finances

Managing finances is a cornerstone of success for any electronics store. It involves a multifaceted approach encompassing budgeting, cash flow management, and strategic financial decision-making.

To start, creating a detailed budget is crucial. Identify all expenses, including rent, inventory, utilities, salaries, marketing, and any other operational costs. A clear budget provides a roadmap for spending and helps in monitoring expenses.

Cash flow management is paramount. In an electronics store where inventory turnover is significant, keeping a healthy cash flow ensures the ability to restock products and cover ongoing expenses. It involves efficient inventory management to minimize tied-up capital and negotiating favorable payment terms with suppliers.

Implementing robust accounting practices is fundamental. Accurate record-keeping allows for better financial analysis and decision-making. Utilize accounting software or hire professionals to maintain meticulous records of income, expenses, and profits.

Strategic pricing is a financial strategy that can significantly impact the bottom line. Determine pricing that covers costs, ensures profitability, and remains competitive in the market. Consider factors like product demand, competitors' prices, and customer expectations.

Investing in technology and tools that streamline financial processes can be a wise decision. Point-of-sale systems that integrate inventory management and sales tracking can provide real-time insights into the store's financial health.

Regular financial reviews and performance assessments are essential. Analyze financial statements to identify trends, assess profitability per product category, and pinpoint areas for cost-saving or revenue enhancement.

Moreover, establishing a contingency fund is prudent. Unexpected expenses or fluctuations in sales can occur, and having reserves can cushion the impact on the store's finances.

Lastly, seeking professional financial advice or consulting with experts in the retail industry can provide valuable insights and strategies for effective financial management in the dynamic and competitive landscape of an electronics store.

Chapter 5:
Store Design and Layout

The design and layout of your computer store play a pivotal role in shaping the customer experience, optimizing efficiency, and driving sales. In this chapter, we will delve into the critical aspects of store design and layout, including store layout considerations, shelving and merchandising strategies, equipment and fixtures, and interior design.

Store Layout Considerations

Designing an effective store layout necessitates careful planning to create a shopping environment that caters to your customers' needs while optimizing sales. Here are several key store layout considerations:

Customer Flow: Plan a layout that guides customers smoothly through the store. Consider placing frequently purchased items towards the entrance to attract attention and encourage exploration deeper into the store. Create clear pathways that make it easy for customers to navigate and find what they need.

Product Placement: Organize products logically based on categories and usage frequency. Group related items together, such as plumbing supplies or electrical tools, to facilitate easy shopping and enhance the customer experience. Highlight popular or seasonal items prominently.

Aisles and Shelving: Optimize aisle width for easy movement and accommodate carts or trolleys. Adjustable shelving allows flexibility to accommodate various product sizes. Ensure shelves are well-stocked, neatly organized, and labeled clearly for effortless browsing.

Checkout Area: Strategically position checkout counters to minimize wait times and create a seamless checkout process. Consider additional displays near the checkout area for last-minute purchases or impulse buys.

Accessibility: Ensure the store layout is accessible to all customers, including those with disabilities. Maintain clear pathways, provide ramps or elevators where necessary, and ensure that product displays are reachable for all customers.

Safety and Comfort: Prioritize safety by keeping aisles clear of obstructions, ensuring proper lighting, and maintaining a clean and hazard-free environment. Incorporate comfortable waiting areas for customers and seating for those in need of assistance or consultation.

Flexibility and Adaptability: Design the layout with flexibility in mind to accommodate changes in inventory, seasonal displays, or promotional setups. This adaptability allows for easy modifications to meet evolving customer needs and store requirements.

Testing and Demonstration Areas: Consider allocating space for customers to test tools or equipment. Providing demonstration areas enhances customer engagement and allows for hands-on experience, influencing purchase decisions.

Employee Accessibility: Design employee workstations strategically to facilitate efficient restocking, inventory management, and customer assistance. Ensure staff areas are easily accessible but not obstructive to customer flow.

By considering these store layout considerations, you can create an inviting, efficient, and customer-friendly environment that maximizes sales potential and enhances the overall shopping experience at your computer store.

Shelving and Merchandising

Optimizing the layout and presentation of products is crucial in a computer store to entice customers, maximize space, and boost sales. Employ these strategies to achieve these objectives:

Shelving Selection: Choose shelves that accommodate your store's range of products. Adjustable shelves offer flexibility for varying item sizes, while specialized shelving (such as gridwall systems or pegboards) caters to specific merchandise categories like accessories or peripherals.

Product Arrangement: Organize products logically and visually appealingly. Group similar items together using categories or themes to guide customers. Employ clear signage and labels for easy navigation and identification.

Planogram Development: Create a planogram—a visual representation of shelf displays—to optimize space and drive sales. Strategically place products for maximum visibility and customer appeal.

Eye-Catching Placement: Position high-demand or premium items at eye level to capture customer attention. Prime shelf space tends to attract more interest and prompt purchases.

Cross-Promotion: Pair complementary products together to encourage additional purchases. Display accessories alongside main items (e.g., mice with laptops) to prompt customers to buy related products in one visit.

Seasonal Showcases: Utilize shelves and displays to highlight seasonal or promotional items. Rotate merchandise according to seasons or upcoming events to meet customer demands.

Visual Presentation: Use visual elements like color schemes, appealing displays, and well-organized shelves to create an inviting shopping atmosphere. Employ informative signage or demo areas to educate customers about products.

Inventory Maintenance: Regularly restock shelves to ensure items are available and well-presented. Employ inventory management systems to monitor stock levels and avoid shortages.

Safety Precautions: Ensure shelves are stable, properly maintained, and comply with safety standards to prevent accidents. Avoid overcrowding to maintain a safe shopping environment.

Employee Training: Train staff in effective merchandising techniques and the importance of a well-organized store. Empower them to assist customers and provide product knowledge.

Implementing effective shelving and merchandising practices not only enhances the shopping experience but also drives sales, fosters customer satisfaction, and cultivates a positive in-store ambiance for your computer store.

Equipment and Fixtures

When setting up your computer store, having the right equipment and fixtures is vital for smooth operations and a welcoming shopping space. Here's a rundown of essential items to consider:

Shelving and Display Units: Invest in sturdy, adaptable shelves to showcase a range of products. Adjustable shelves accommodate various item sizes, while racking systems are perfect for storing bulkier items like computer peripherals or components.

Display Options: Use pegboards, gridwall systems, or slatwall panels to display accessories or smaller items effectively. These fixtures provide flexibility in arranging merchandise and optimizing your store's layout.

Point-of-Sale (POS) System: Implement a reliable POS system for efficient sales management and inventory tracking. Choose one that suits your store's scale, integrating features like inventory control and reporting tools.

Storage Solutions: Organize smaller computer items with bins, drawers, or labeled cabinets for easy access and inventory management.

Checkout Equipment: Set up user-friendly cash registers or POS terminals equipped with barcode scanners, receipt printers, and card payment facilities for seamless transactions.

Security Measures: Install security cameras, alarms, and visible deterrents to protect your store and merchandise. Adequate lighting also helps deter theft.

Material Handling Tools: Consider hand trucks, forklifts, or carts to efficiently handle heavy items, making stocking and organizing merchandise easier.

Signage and Promotion: Use signage, banners, and displays for product promotion and pricing information. Clear and informative signage enhances the shopping experience.

Workstations: Equip workstations with necessary tools for customer service and store operations. Tools like saws, drills, or measuring equipment should be readily available.

Lighting Arrangement: Install appropriate lighting fixtures to create an inviting atmosphere. Ambient, task, and accent lighting can highlight products and enhance the overall shopping environment.

Choosing durable, functional, and visually appealing equipment tailored to your store's layout and customer needs is crucial for a successful computer store. Make sure these items align with your operational requirements to create a well-equipped and customer-friendly establishment.

Interior Design

Designing the interior of a computer store is like crafting an experience for shoppers, where every element contributes to their comfort and convenience. The layout is a critical aspect, ensuring that aisles, displays, and checkouts are strategically placed for easy navigation and efficient operations.

Lighting plays a significant role, creating a welcoming atmosphere and showcasing products effectively. The right balance of natural and artificial light contributes not only to visibility but also to the overall sense of cleanliness and safety in the store.

Colors subtly influence the mood of the store. Warm and inviting tones create a comfortable ambiance, while strategic color use can highlight promotions or specific sections. Branding elements and signage add to the visual appeal and help customers easily recognize and navigate through the store.

Product displays are crucial for both aesthetics and sales. Well-organized shelves, attractive endcap displays, and eye-catching promotions draw attention to products and encourage spontaneous purchases. Grouping similar items together enhances the convenience of the shopping experience.

Checkout counters are central points of customer interaction. Designing these areas for efficiency and customer satisfaction, with features like express lanes and well-organized impulse-buy sections, contributes to a positive overall impression.

Incorporating technology adds a modern touch to computer store design. Digital signage, interactive displays, and mobile checkout options not only enhance the store's appearance but also engage customers and make their shopping experience more convenient.

Safety and accessibility are paramount considerations in computer store interior design. Ensuring adequate space for wheelchair users, clear emergency exits, and a well-designed customer service area contribute to an inclusive and secure shopping environment.

In essence, the interior design of a computer store is a blend of functionality and aesthetics, aimed at creating a pleasant and efficient shopping experience. From the layout to lighting, colors, displays, and technology, each element plays a role in shaping the atmosphere and influencing customer behavior for the success of the store.

The design and layout of your computer store are critical elements that influence customer experience, operational efficiency, and sales performance. By carefully considering store layout, shelving and merchandising strategies, equipment and fixtures, and interior design, you can create a shopping environment that attracts customers, encourages sales, and sets your computer store apart from the competition.

Chapter 6:
Product Selection and Suppliers

The success of your computer store heavily relies on the products you offer and the relationships you build with suppliers. In this chapter, we will delve into the critical aspects of product selection and suppliers, including building relationships with suppliers, managing inventory effectively and implementing pricing strategies,.

Product Selection

When managing a computer store, focusing on both customer satisfaction and sales stands as paramount. The success of sales relies heavily on understanding the customers and the products you offer.

While you can't dictate customer choices, steering sales can involve offering products that feel custom-tailored to their desires and needs. The real question emerges: how do you determine the right products to feature? The starting point involves planning to cater to customer needs, ensuring your inventory aligns with what they seek.

Consider Meeting Customer Needs
Except for impulse purchases, your customers likely arrive with specific wants or requirements. As a retailer, your goal is to curate and select products that fulfill these needs. If customers frequent your store for gifts, stocking cleaning supplies might not align with their expectations, despite the practicality of these items in everyday life.

While you might fancy a niche product, the crux is understanding its marketability. Numerous strategies exist to cater to customer needs, each catering to unique demands. Striking a balance between products you favor and those that sell well involves analyzing popular items with a strong return on investment.

Predicting sales success and identifying what won't sell can be facilitated through research.

Conduct Thorough Market Research
Conducting market research holds immense significance in product selection. Understanding consumer behavior, preferences, and purchasing patterns helps identify your target audience. Key factors in this research include demographics, customer personas, market trends, and location specificity. For instance, if your store is close to a college campus, catering to the interests of young adults by offering apartment decor, tech gadgets, loungewear, and accessories could align well with their preferences.

Analyze Customer Demand
Competitive analysis serves as another avenue to gauge customer needs. Observing what your competitors sell, along with trends both in-store and online, aids in understanding the market landscape.

Competitive research is akin to window shopping, examining what's trending or most sought after on platforms like Amazon or Etsy. This exploration resembles a mental shopping spree, offering insights into current customer demands.

Choose Products for Your Store
After conducting thorough market research and analysis, you'll possess the insights necessary to guide your product selection process. Keep in mind, choosing the appropriate products for a laptop store is crucial for drawing in customers and securing success. Here's a guide on product selection:

Diverse Range: Offer a diverse selection of laptops to cater to different customer needs. Include various brands, sizes, and specifications, such as gaming laptops, ultrabooks, business laptops, and 2-in-1 convertible models.

Latest Models: Stay updated with the latest releases from reputable manufacturers. Stocking the newest models ensures your store remains competitive and appeals to customers seeking cutting-edge technology.

Different Price Points: Have laptops available at various price points to accommodate different budgets. This includes entry-level, mid-range, and high-end options, allowing customers to find something suitable for their financial constraints.

Specialized Features: Highlight laptops with specialized features, such as long battery life, powerful processors, high-resolution displays, or lightweight designs. Tailoring your selection to specific user needs can attract niche markets.

Variety of Operating Systems: Offer laptops with different operating systems like Windows, macOS, and Chrome OS. Providing options ensures customers can choose based on their preferences and familiarity with specific platforms.

Accessories and Add-Ons: Include a selection of accessories like laptop bags, cases, external storage, docking stations, and peripherals. Upselling these add-ons can increase sales and enhance the customer's overall experience.

Demo Units and Display Models: Have demo units or display models available for customers to test and experience firsthand. This hands-on approach helps customers make informed decisions and builds trust in the products.

Warranties and Support Services: Partner with manufacturers or provide your own warranty and support services. Offering extended warranties or tech support can incentivize customers to choose your store over competitors.

Customer Feedback and Trends: Pay attention to customer feedback and market trends. Analyze which models sell well and which features customers prefer. This data can guide future purchasing decisions.

Stay Flexible: Continuously evaluate and adjust your product selection based on market demand, emerging technologies, and customer preferences. Flexibility is key in adapting to the ever-evolving laptop market.

By carefully curating a diverse range of laptops, keeping abreast of market trends, and catering to various customer needs, your laptop store can become a go-to destination for tech enthusiasts and everyday consumers alike.

Building Relationships with Suppliers

Building strong and lasting relationships with suppliers is a crucial aspect of running a successful computer store. These partnerships not only ensure a steady supply of products but also offer various benefits that can positively impact your business.

Firstly, effective communication is the foundation of any strong supplier relationship. Open and transparent lines of communication foster trust and understanding between you and your suppliers. Regularly discussing your needs, concerns, and expectations can lead to better collaboration and problem-solving when issues arise.

Another key element in building supplier relationships is reliability. Consistently meeting payment deadlines and honoring agreements demonstrates your commitment and reliability as a business partner. This reliability can lead to better terms, such as discounts, extended credit, or priority access to high-demand products.

Mutual respect is essential. Treating your suppliers with respect and professionalism, just as you expect from them, creates a positive working environment. This can lead to better customer service, faster response times, and a willingness to go the extra mile to support your store. Building trust takes time and effort. One way to foster trust is by sharing your business plans and goals with your suppliers. When suppliers understand your vision, they can tailor their offerings and support to align with your objectives.

Collaboration is also key in supplier relationships. Engaging in joint initiatives, such as marketing campaigns or product development, can be mutually beneficial. This not only strengthens the bond but can also lead to innovative solutions and increased sales.

Regularly reviewing and evaluating your supplier relationships is vital. Assess the quality of products, delivery timelines, and the overall value they bring to your business. If issues arise, address them promptly and constructively, seeking solutions that benefit both parties.

Building relationships with suppliers is not just about transactions; it's about creating partnerships that benefit both your computer store and your suppliers. Open communication, reliability, mutual respect, trust, collaboration, and regular evaluation are the pillars of successful supplier relationships. Investing time and effort in nurturing these relationships can contribute significantly to your store's success and sustainability.

Managing Inventory

Having secured suppliers and goods starts coming in, you would have to manage your inventories. Effective inventory management involves several key components that work together to ensure you have the right products in the right quantities at the right times.

One fundamental aspect of inventory management is accurate tracking. This entails keeping detailed records of your inventory levels, product turnover rates, and reorder points. Utilizing modern inventory management software can streamline this process, providing real-time insights into your stock levels and helping you make informed decisions.

Strategic purchasing is another crucial element. It involves ordering products in quantities that align with your store's demand patterns and sales trends. Analyzing historical sales data can help you forecast future demand and avoid overstocking or understocking items, which can tie up capital or result in missed sales opportunities.

Categorizing your inventory into different classifications can also be beneficial. Items can be categorized as fast-moving, slow-moving, or non-moving, allowing you to allocate resources more effectively. Fast-moving items may require frequent restocking, while slow-moving or non-moving items may warrant different management strategies, such as promotions or clearance sales.

Implementing inventory control measures can help prevent issues like theft, damlage, or obsolescence. This can involve using security systems, monitoring expiration dates, and regularly inspecting inventory for damage or discrepancies.

Regularly conducting physical inventory counts is essential for accuracy. Periodic audits ensure that your recorded inventory levels align with the actual quantities on your shelves and in your storage areas. It's a time-consuming process, but the benefits in terms of accurate record-keeping and minimizing discrepancies are invaluable.

Effective inventory management also involves developing relationships with your suppliers. Establishing clear communication channels, negotiating favorable terms, and collaborating on supply chain efficiencies can help ensure a reliable and cost-effective flow of products into your store.

Finally, embracing technology can significantly enhance your inventory management efforts. Utilizing inventory management software, barcode scanning systems, and automated reorder triggers can streamline processes, reduce errors, and improve overall efficiency. Managing inventory in a computer store requires a multifaceted approach that encompasses accurate tracking, strategic purchasing, categorization, control measures, physical counts, supplier relationships, and the integration of technology. By effectively managing your inventory, you can optimize your store's operations, maximize profitability, and provide a satisfying shopping experience for your customers.

Pricing Strategies

Pricing strategies serve as essential tools for boosting product sales and optimizing profits within a computer store. Recognizing the significance of these strategies is paramount as they profoundly impact customer behavior, subsequently influencing the store's profitability and overall revenue. Finding the right equilibrium between competitive pricing, which attracts customers, and sustaining profit margins is vital for the long-term success of the business. This delicate balance ensures both customer satisfaction and financial stability, fostering sustained growth and prosperity for the computer store.

Here's how we can adapt that information for a computer store:

Dynamic pricing is a powerful tool for your computer store, allowing you to adjust prices in real time based on various factors like demand, competition, and seasonal trends. This strategy enables you to optimize prices according to market conditions, ensuring competitiveness and maximizing value capture. Think of your favorite ride-sharing app — it's a prime example of how dynamic pricing responds to changing demand. Implementing this approach can help your computer store stay agile and align prices with market dynamics, enhancing competitiveness and meeting customer demand effectively.

One common pricing strategy is value-based pricing, where the store adds a markup to the cost of goods to determine the selling price. This approach ensures that the store covers its expenses and generates a profit. However, it may not consider market demand or competition, potentially leading to overpricing or underpricing.

Competitive pricing is another widely used strategy. In this approach, computer stores set their prices in line with or slightly below the prices offered by their competitors. This strategy aims to attract price-conscious shoppers and maintain competitiveness in the market. Regular price monitoring and adjustments are essential to stay competitive.

Promotional pricing is a valuable tool to drive sales and customer loyalty. It includes strategies like discounts, buy-one-get-one-free (BOGO) offers, and loyalty programs. These promotions attract shoppers looking for deals and can boost sales for specific products or categories.

Psychological pricing tactics leverage consumer psychology to influence purchasing decisions. These tactics include using pricing endings like "$499" instead of rounding to the nearest dollar or emphasizing savings by showing a "discounted" price alongside the regular price. Such tactics create a perception of value and can lead to increased sales.

Price elasticity is an essential concept in pricing strategy. It measures how sensitive customer demand is to changes in price. Products with inelastic demand, such as essential tools, can tolerate price increases without significant decreases in sales. However, products with elastic demand, like luxury items, are more sensitive to price changes.

Strategic pricing should consider the overall store positioning and target market. A store focusing on premium or standard products may employ higher pricing to align with its brand image, while a store catering to budget-conscious shoppers may adopt a more aggressive pricing strategy.

Penetration Pricing is a strategic approach utilized by computer stores when entering a new market. In this method, aggressive initial pricing is set for the products on offer. By presenting introductory lower prices, the store aims to entice price-sensitive buyers and establish a customer base seeking better value in products. However, it's essential to view this pricing strategy from a long-term perspective, ensuring profitability and sustainability over time.

In your computer store, setting prices is an ongoing process that demands constant attention, analysis, and adjustment. By employing test and learn methodologies, you can experiment with diverse pricing strategies, assess their impact, and refine your approach accordingly. This iterative approach allows you to continuously improve and adapt your pricing strategies to the ever-changing market dynamics.

It's crucial to stay abreast of industry trends and keep a keen eye on competitor activities. Regularly monitoring your competitors' pricing strategies, promotional campaigns, and market trends offers valuable insights and opportunities for adjusting your pricing strategy. This competitive intelligence empowers you to make informed pricing decisions, ensuring your computer store maintains a competitive edge in the market.

Utilizing effective pricing strategies like dynamic pricing, value-based pricing, psychological pricing, and penetration pricing can work wonders. These strategies help attract customers, add value to your offerings, and ultimately boost your profitability. It's crucial to tap into data-driven insights, keep an eye on market trends, and stay updated with industry shifts to consistently refine your pricing decisions.

Pricing isn't a one-time fix; it's an ongoing journey that demands flexibility and a bit of experimentation. By adopting these retail pricing strategies, computer stores can adapt better to customer demands and the ever-changing market conditions. It's all about positioning your business for growth and success in this dynamic retail landscape.

Chapter 7:
Staffing and Management

Effective staffing and management are fundamental to the success of your computer store. In this chapter, we will explore the key components of staffing and managing your computer store, including the hiring and training of employees, the creation of employee policies, scheduling and shift management, and performance evaluation.

Hiring and Training Employees

When establishing a computer store, having the right team of employees is crucial for providing excellent customer service, managing operations, and fostering a positive shopping experience. Consider the following roles and personnel needed:

Store Manager: An experienced store manager oversees daily operations, manages staff, handles inventory, ensures customer satisfaction, and implements business strategies. They play a pivotal role in maintaining the store's efficiency and profitability.

Sales Associates: Frontline sales associates assist customers, provide product information, process transactions, and maintain a neat and organized sales floor. They should possess excellent communication skills, product knowledge, and a customer-oriented approach.

Cashiers: Efficient cashiers handle transactions, process payments accurately, and provide customers with a positive checkout experience. They should be proficient in operating cash registers and handling various payment methods.

Inventory Manager: An inventory manager oversees stock levels, conducts inventory audits, manages orders, and ensures accurate tracking of merchandise. Their role is crucial in maintaining adequate inventory levels and preventing stock shortages.

Technical Experts: Employ individuals with specialized knowledge in computer, tools, or specific trades. These experts can provide valuable advice to customers, offer guidance on product selection, and assist with technical queries.

Customer Service Representatives: Customer service representatives handle inquiries, resolve issues, and address customer concerns promptly and professionally. They serve as the liaison between customers and the store, ensuring a high level of satisfaction.

Maintenance Staff: Maintenance personnel ensure the store premises are clean, well-maintained, and adhere to safety standards. They handle repairs, upkeep of equipment, and manage facilities to create a safe and pleasant environment for customers and employees.

The process of hiring and training employees begins with a well-planned recruitment process aimed at attracting candidates who align with your store's values and customer service standards. Utilizing various channels such as online job boards, local newspapers, and social media, you can advertise job openings effectively. Additionally, consider hosting in-person or virtual job fairs to engage potential candidates.

Once you've identified suitable candidates, a rigorous selection process, including resume screening, interviews, reference checks, and skills assessments, ensures that you select employees who not only possess the necessary qualifications but also fit well within your store's culture. When recruiting, prioritize individuals with relevant industry experience, a customer-centric attitude, strong communication skills, and a willingness to learn and adapt. Following the hiring process, invest in comprehensive training programs that encompass on-the-job training and formal training sessions. These programs ensure that your staff members are well-versed in product offerings, customer service expectations, safety protocols, and store policies.

Creating Employee Policies

Establishing clear and comprehensive employee guidelines is key to a smooth and happy workplace. Start by crafting an employee handbook that serves as a go-to guide for your team. This handbook should cover everything from work schedules and dress code to attendance rules and performance expectations. Be sure to outline a code of conduct that lays out expected behavior and ethical standards for everyone, stressing the importance of respecting both customers and fellow colleagues.

It's crucial to implement policies against discrimination and harassment to foster a safe, inclusive environment. Make sure to clearly explain reporting procedures so that all employees know their rights and how they're protected.

Safety and health policies should be a top priority, making sure you're in line with local regulations and emphasizing the importance of a safe work environment. When it comes to compensation, lay out everything transparently—wage rates, overtime policies, benefits, and perks. And don't forget about attendance and punctuality guidelines, including how to request time off or report absences.

Additionally, it's essential to create policies for handling conflicts, providing a fair and confidential process for employees to address any issues with management or coworkers. Lastly, educate your team on respecting customer privacy and confidentiality, making sure they're clear on how to handle sensitive information appropriately.

Performance Evaluation

Performance evaluation is a pivotal aspect of managing your computer store staff. Define key performance metrics for various roles within the store, including sales targets, customer service ratings, and productivity goals. Provide ongoing feedback to employees, helping them understand their strengths and areas for improvement. Encourage open dialogue and constructive feedback as part of your organizational culture.

Conduct regular performance reviews or evaluations to assess employee performance against established metrics and goals. Set aside dedicated time for these evaluations and involve employees in goal setting to align their individual objectives with the store's overall objectives. Recognize and reward outstanding performance through incentive programs, awards, or bonuses to motivate and retain high-performing employees.

Moreover, discuss career development opportunities with employees and provide guidance on how they can advance within the organization. Offer training and support for career growth, demonstrating your commitment to their professional development. In cases where employees are not meeting performance expectations, develop performance improvement plans that outline specific steps for improvement. Offer support and resources to help employees succeed while also being prepared to take appropriate action, including termination, if performance issues persist despite efforts to address them.

Managing staffing and employee performance is an ongoing process that demands attention to detail, effective communication, and a commitment to fostering a positive work environment. By hiring and training employees effectively, creating clear policies, managing schedules efficiently, and conducting performance evaluations, you can build a motivated and capable team that contributes significantly to the success of your computer store.

Chapter 8:
Marketing and Promotion

In the computer industry, a well-crafted marketing and promotion strategy is essential to attract and retain customers, create a strong brand presence, and drive sales. In this chapter, we will explore the key components of effective marketing and promotion for your computer store, including developing a marketing plan, establishing your store's branding and image, implementing advertising and promotion strategies, and utilizing loyalty programs to foster customer loyalty and engagement.

Developing a Marketing Plan

A marketing plan serves as the guiding blueprint for a computer store's promotional activities, providing a structured approach to achieving desired outcomes. To develop a comprehensive marketing plan, several key steps should be followed.

Conducting Market Research

Market research forms the cornerstone of an effective marketing strategy for your computer store. It's the vital process of gathering information that unveils the thoughts, purchasing behaviors, and geographical presence of your customers.

This research isn't just about understanding your customers; it's also a tool to craft an initial sales forecast, track market shifts, and keenly observe your competitors' actions.

By delving into market research, you'll gain valuable insights into what drives your customers' decisions, where they are located, and how they engage with computer products. This knowledge becomes the bedrock upon which you can build a robust marketing strategy that resonates with your target audience, identifies growth opportunities, and sets your store apart from the competition.

Whether it's analyzing buying patterns, gauging customer preferences, or staying updated on industry trends, market research empowers your computer store to make informed decisions and stay ahead in a dynamic market landscape.

Profiling Your Target Markets
Attempting to reach everyone with your computer products can drain resources and yield minimal impact. Instead, focusing your marketing efforts through segmentation can be a game-changer. By grouping potential customers based on specific characteristics, you can refine and tailor your marketing strategies for maximum effectiveness.

Here are key segmentation factors to consider:

Geography: Understand where your customers live and work. This insight helps tailor your marketing approach to specific regions or areas.

Demographics: Consider gender, age, education level, occupation, and income. These details paint a clearer picture of your customer base and aid in crafting targeted messages.

Behavior: Why would they use your products? What draws them to your brand? Understanding usage rates and their preferred information sources guides how you communicate and engage with them.

Lifestyle and Values: Delve into their family situation, values, hobbies, and interests. Knowing these aspects helps align your marketing messages with what matters most to them.

Your ideal target market should not only require your computer offerings but also be willing to invest in them. Understanding their needs, preferences, and behaviors empowers you to tailor your marketing efforts effectively. By honing in on specific customer segments, your computer store can deliver tailored solutions that resonate deeply with these diverse groups, fostering stronger connections and driving more impactful results.

Crafting Your Unique Selling Proposition (USP)
Your computer store's USP is the distinctive factor that sets you apart from competitors and entices customers to choose you over others. It's the essence of what makes your business shine in a crowded market. Defining and effectively communicating your USP is key to captivating potential customers.

To develop your USP, consider the following:

Passion for Products and Services: What excites you the most about your offerings? Your genuine enthusiasm often translates into a unique selling point. Whether it's the quality, variety, or innovation, conveying your passion can be magnetic.

Specialized Skills and Knowledge: Identify the unique expertise or knowledge your team possesses. This could be technical know-how, expert guidance, or a deep understanding of specific products—factors that differentiate you from the competition.

Customer Draw: Why do customers choose you over others? Understanding this helps define your USP. Whether it's exceptional service, a loyalty program, or a personalized approach, pinpoint what consistently attracts customers to your store.

Customer Benefits: Highlight the tangible advantages your customers gain by choosing your products or services. Whether it's convenience, reliability, cost-effectiveness, or solving specific problems, emphasize how customers benefit from their association with your store.

Key Messaging: When describing your business to strangers, what aspects do you emphasize? These points often align with your USP. Whether it's outstanding customer support, exclusive product lines, or a commitment to quality, these aspects become pivotal in shaping your USP's narrative.

By analyzing these aspects, you can distill your computer store's unique strengths into a compelling USP. This proposition becomes the backbone of your marketing efforts, guiding your messaging, and resonating strongly with potential customers, ultimately setting you apart and driving customer loyalty and engagement.

Developing Your Business Brand
Creating a brand for your computer store is a comprehensive endeavor that involves more than just the visual elements like logos and colors. It's about establishing a meaningful connection with your target audience. A well-crafted brand goes beyond surface-level aesthetics; it's a means to communicate your core values, your identity, and what customers can expect from your store.

Choose Your Marketing Media
When it comes to marketing your computer store, the array of avenues available can be overwhelming. However, it's crucial to align your choices with your target audience to maximize their effectiveness.

Consider these options:

Business Website: Establishing an online presence through a website allows potential customers to explore your offerings, services, and values. It's a digital storefront that can attract and engage customers.

Social Media: Platforms like Facebook, Instagram, or LinkedIn offer opportunities to connect with your audience on a more personal level. Engaging content and interaction can build a community around your brand.

Blogging: Creating informative and valuable content through a blog can position your store as an authority in the computer industry. It's a way to share expertise and attract customers seeking guidance.

Brochures and Flyers: Tangible marketing materials can be effective in local promotions or events. They provide a physical reminder of your store and offerings.

Networking Events: Engaging in industry-related events or local gatherings can help forge connections and establish your store within the community.

Print Advertising: Traditional print media, like newspapers or magazines, can still reach a specific demographic effectively, especially in localized markets.

Word of Mouth: Encourage satisfied customers to spread the word about your store. Positive recommendations can be a powerful driver for new customers.

Cold Calling: Direct outreach can be effective in B2B sales or when targeting specific customer segments. It's a proactive way to introduce your store and offerings.

Email Marketing: Sending targeted and personalized emails can nurture customer relationships, share promotions, and keep your store top-of-mind.

By understanding your target audience's preferences and behaviors, you can select the most fitting marketing avenues for your computer store. Each avenue offers distinct opportunities to engage with customers, amplify your brand, and drive sales, so tailoring your approach to match your audience's preferences is key to maximizing your marketing efforts.

Establishing Goals and Allocating Budget for Your Marketing
Defining clear and concise marketing goals is pivotal for guiding your computer store's growth. These goals should adhere to the SMART criteria—specific, measurable, attainable, relevant, and time-based.

Consider setting goals such as increasing website traffic by a certain percentage, boosting social media engagement, or enhancing sales of specific product categories within a defined timeframe. These objectives provide direction and allow for effective evaluation of your marketing efforts.

For a computer store, these SMART objectives could encompass various goals:

- Increasing Sales: Define a specific percentage increase in sales within a set timeframe.
- Expanding Market Share: Set a goal to capture a certain percentage of the local computer market within a year.

- Launching a New Store Location: Outline specific steps and targets to successfully launch a new store, including a timeline for pre-launch marketing, opening day sales, and post-launch growth.

Allocating a budget is equally crucial. Your marketing budget needs to encompass various elements essential for promoting your computer store effectively. It should cover:

Website Development and Maintenance: Investing in a professional and user-friendly website is fundamental. Regular maintenance ensures it remains up-to-date and functional.

Search Engine Optimization (SEO) Strategy: Optimizing your online presence to rank higher in search engine results is vital for visibility. Allocate resources for SEO tools and strategies to enhance your store's online discoverability.

Branding Design: Designing a compelling brand identity, including logos, color schemes, and visual elements that resonate with your target audience.

Printing of Promotional Material: Costs related to producing business cards, brochures, signage, and other promotional materials that represent your store's image.

Advertising Costs: Funding for advertising campaigns across various platforms, whether digital, print, or local media.

Donations and Sponsorships: Consider community involvement through donations or sponsorships that align with your brand values and foster positive relationships.

Staff for Marketing Activities: Allocating resources for employing or training staff dedicated to marketing activities, ensuring a focused approach towards achieving marketing goals.

By establishing SMART goals and earmarking a comprehensive budget covering these critical marketing elements, your computer store can strategically channel resources towards initiatives that align with your business objectives. This disciplined approach enhances the effectiveness of your marketing endeavors, leading to tangible results and the sustained growth of your store.

Nurturing Your Valued Customers
Your customers are the backbone of your computer store's success, making it imperative to prioritize their care and loyalty. Exceptional customer service isn't just a bonus—it's a crucial factor that retains customers and sets you apart from competitors.

Here are strategies to cultivate customer loyalty:

Regular Communication: Engage customers consistently through social media, blogs, or e-newsletters. Providing valuable content and updates keeps your store top-of-mind.

After-Sale Follow-Up: Show your commitment by following up after a sale. Checking in on their satisfaction and offering support builds a lasting impression.

Delivering on Promises: Consistently meeting or exceeding promises made to customers establishes trust and reliability.

Going the Extra Mile: Surprise and delight your customers by providing benefits that surpass their initial expectations. It could be personalized recommendations, exclusive discounts, or exceptional service that leaves a lasting positive impression.

Utilizing Feedback: Embrace feedback and complaints as opportunities to enhance your services. Actively listening and implementing necessary improvements demonstrate your dedication to customer satisfaction.

Listening Intently: Take the time to genuinely listen to your customers. Understanding their needs and concerns helps tailor your services to meet their expectations effectively.

Staff Training: Invest in training your staff in customer service and sales processes. Equipping them with the skills to engage customers positively enhances the overall experience.

By implementing these strategies, your computer store can foster a loyal customer base. Consistently providing exceptional service, actively listening to feedback, and going beyond expectations help create a strong bond with customers. This dedication not only encourages repeat business but also turns satisfied customers into enthusiastic advocates, driving positive word-of-mouth and contributing significantly to your store's long-term success.

Monitoring and Reviewing Marketing Effort
Regularly monitoring and assessing your marketing initiatives is crucial to ensure they align with your goals and deliver the desired outcomes, such as increased sales or heightened brand visibility. Initially, it's recommended to review your marketing plan every three months to ensure your activities are in sync with your overall strategy. As your business matures, consider reviewing the plan when introducing new products/services, encountering new competitors, or facing industry-related challenges.

Monitoring activities involves various assessments, such as regularly analyzing sales figures (monthly) or tracking customer engagement during advertising campaigns. Leveraging free analytic tools enables you to evaluate the effectiveness of your social media or website campaigns.

By routinely evaluating the performance of your marketing efforts, you can gain valuable insights into what strategies are yielding positive results and which ones may need adjustments. This process helps in optimizing your marketing activities, reallocating resources to high-performing channels, and refining strategies to better resonate with your target audience.

Additionally, staying vigilant regarding shifts in the market, new industry trends, or changes in customer behavior enables you to adapt swiftly. By continuously monitoring and reviewing your marketing plan, your computer store remains agile and responsive to evolving market conditions, ensuring sustained growth and success in the competitive landscape.

Branding and Store Image

Branding encompasses more than just a logo and a catchy slogan; it represents the essence of your computer store's identity. Building a strong brand image is not only essential for setting your store apart from competitors but also for fostering customer trust and leaving a lasting impression. To create a compelling brand identity, follow these essential steps:

Define Your Brand: The process begins by clearly defining your store's values, mission, and vision. What is it that you want your computer store to stand for, and what unique qualities will distinguish it from others in the market?

Logo and Visual Identity: Craft a memorable logo and visual identity that align with your brand's personality and values. It's crucial to ensure consistency in these branding elements across all marketing materials and in-store signage.

Store Layout and Design: The interior design and layout of your store should seamlessly align with your brand image. The atmosphere, color schemes, and decor should vividly convey your brand's values and resonate with your target audience.

Customer Experience: Delivering a consistent and exceptional customer experience is pivotal to upholding your brand promise. Train your staff to embody your brand values in their interactions with customers, creating a lasting impression.

Brand Messaging: Develop compelling brand messaging that effectively communicates your store's unique selling points and resonates with your intended audience. Maintain the consistency of this messaging across all communication channels.

Brand Voice: Cultivate a consistent brand voice that reflects your brand's personality. Whether it's a friendly, informative, or humorous tone, ensure that it remains aligned with your brand image.

Community Engagement: Actively engage with the local community and support causes that align with your brand values. Sponsoring local events, participating in charity initiatives, or contributing to environmental efforts can enhance your brand's reputation and foster a sense of community.

Feedback and Adaptation: Continuously seek feedback from your customers to gain insights into their perceptions of your brand. Be willing to adapt and evolve your brand identity in response to changing customer preferences and market trends.

In essence, branding and store image creation involve a holistic approach that encompasses visual identity, messaging, atmosphere, and customer experience. By meticulously crafting and nurturing your brand, you can establish a distinct and memorable identity in the computer market, leading to increased customer loyalty and trust.

Promoting Your Store

Getting the word out about your computer store is essential, and fortunately, today's landscape offers a myriad of promotional avenues. Traditional business promotion methods remain effective, but the surge of social media has opened up a wealth of new marketing opportunities. Embracing digital marketing and social media can present affordable and accessible advertising options for your store. Here's how to leverage these tools to promote your business effectively:

Maximize Local Exposure

Harness the power of local listings by ensuring your computer store is listed on Google—a modern-day equivalent to the classic yellow pages. Registering your business with Google offers numerous advantages, allowing potential customers to effortlessly locate your store's address and operating hours.

Here's why setting up a Google My Business account is pivotal:

Enhanced Visibility: A Google My Business account significantly boosts your store's online visibility. When users search for computer stores in your area, your business will appear prominently in search results, increasing your chances of attracting local customers.

Ease of Access: Providing essential information such as your store's location, hours of operation, contact details, and even directions on Google Maps simplifies the process for customers to find and reach your store easily.

Customer Engagement: Google My Business facilitates customer engagement by enabling customers to post reviews and ratings of your computer store. Positive reviews can enhance your store's reputation and influence potential customers' decisions.

Free Advertising: Utilizing Google My Business is essentially a form of free advertising. It extends your store's reach without incurring additional costs, making it a cost-effective way to increase your store's visibility online.

By setting up a Google My Business account, your computer store can leverage the vast reach of Google's search engine to connect with local customers actively seeking computer solutions. This simple yet powerful tool not only enhances your store's visibility but also facilitates customer engagement and trust, ultimately driving foot traffic and boosting your store's success in the local market.

Create a Truthworthy Website
Establishing a reliable online presence is vital for your computer store. Your website should serve as a comprehensive hub showcasing your services, products, and the essence of your computer ethos. It's not just about listing services; it's about conveying your computer philosophy. Offer a seamless booking platform and foster communication with customers. Remember, your website often forms the initial impression of your store, so ensure it mirrors your brand values. Explore top computer store websites for inspiration on how to best represent your business online.

Enhance Your Website with SEO Optimization

Boosting your computer store's online visibility begins with optimizing your website's search engine optimization (SEO). SEO is the key to securing higher rankings in Google searches, making it easier for potential customers to discover your business online. While integrating relevant keywords across your web pages and blog posts is vital, effective SEO involves more than just keyword usage.

To optimize your website's performance on search engines, consider these steps:

Keyword Integration: Strategically incorporate relevant keywords throughout your website's content, ensuring they align with the products, services, and solutions your computer store offers. Use tools or online resources to identify high-impact keywords for your industry.

Content Quality: Focus on creating high-quality, informative content that addresses common queries or issues within the computer and home improvement sphere. Well-crafted content not only engages visitors but also attracts search engine attention.

Technical Optimization: Ensure your website is technically sound by optimizing loading speeds, mobile responsiveness, and user experience. A seamless browsing experience enhances your site's ranking potential.

Research and Learning: Expand your knowledge by exploring online resources or educational materials dedicated to mastering SEO techniques. Understanding the nuances of effective SEO practices can significantly impact your website's performance.

Professional Assistance: Consider hiring an SEO agency or consultant specialized in optimizing websites. Their expertise can offer tailored strategies to enhance your site's SEO, saving time and ensuring effective results.

By embracing SEO best practices, your computer store's website can rise through search engine rankings, attracting more organic traffic and potential customers. A well-optimized website not only improves visibility but also establishes credibility and trust among online users, ultimately contributing to the success and growth of your computer store in the competitive digital landscape.

Leveraging Social Media
Social media has evolved from a mere option to a crucial necessity for businesses. These platforms offer a dynamic space to inform, attract, and actively engage with your audience. Setting up a business account on most social media sites is entirely free, making it an incredibly cost-effective means of advertising for your computer store. While creating paid posts and other forms of social media ads require an investment, the initial setup remains accessible to all.

By establishing a presence on platforms like Facebook, Instagram, Twitter, or LinkedIn, your computer store gains direct access to a vast audience. Through regular posts, stories, and interactions, you can showcase your products, share valuable insights, and build a community around your brand. These platforms also facilitate two-way communication, allowing you to respond promptly to inquiries, address concerns, and foster meaningful connections with your followers.

Paid social media posts and advertisements offer additional advantages by targeting specific demographics, boosting visibility, and driving traffic to your store or website. Though these strategies involve a financial investment, they often yield measurable returns by reaching a tailored audience likely to engage with your computer offerings.

Social media's versatility, accessibility, and potential to reach a wide audience make it an indispensable tool for your computer store's advertising efforts. From establishing brand presence to engaging with customers and running targeted ad campaigns, leveraging social media enables your store to stay competitive, relevant, and connected in today's digital landscape.

Craft Compelling Content
Content stands as the linchpin for amplifying brand awareness and forging connections with your desired audience. Creating compelling and informative content—be it through blogs, video tutorials, or engaging infographics—serves as a powerful tool to showcase your computer store's industry expertise and foster trust among your audience.

Blogs: Share valuable insights, tips, and trends related to computer, home improvement, or DIY projects. Informative blog posts not only exhibit your knowledge but also provide practical guidance that resonates with your audience's interests and needs.

Video Tutorials: Capitalize on the visual medium by producing step-by-step video tutorials showcasing product demonstrations, repair techniques, or innovative uses of computer items. These tutorials not only exhibit your expertise but also serve as valuable resources for your customers.

Infographics: Condense complex information into visually appealing and easily digestible infographics. Highlight product comparisons, maintenance tips, or creative project ideas.

Infographics serve as shareable content that can attract and engage your audience effectively.

By consistently crafting engaging and informative content, your computer store can position itself as a trusted authority within the industry. This approach not only cultivates a deeper connection with your audience but also encourages them to view your store as a go-to resource for their computer needs. As you offer valuable insights and guidance, you simultaneously bolster brand recognition and loyalty, fostering lasting relationships with your customers.

Use High-Quality Visuals
Visual content is the cornerstone of a compelling online presence. For your computer store, investing in high-quality visual content for your website and social media platforms is paramount. In today's digital landscape, users often make decisions based on visuals, making it imperative to showcase your store in its best light.

Consider incorporating photos or videos that spotlight your products, services, facilities, and even your staff. High-resolution images showcasing the details and features of your computer products can captivate potential customers, influencing their buying decisions. Additionally, videos demonstrating the usage or benefits of specific tools or equipment can be incredibly engaging and informative.

On social media, where attention spans are shorter, visually appealing content stands out. Striking images or eye-catching videos are more likely to capture users' attention and encourage engagement. Visuals have the power to convey your store's personality, professionalism, and the value you offer to customers.

Moreover, high-quality visuals not only attract attention but also contribute to establishing credibility and trust. They showcase your dedication to quality and attention to detail, which can resonate positively with your audience.

By prioritizing high-quality visual content across your online platforms, you're not just showcasing your computer store; you're creating an immersive and compelling experience that entices potential customers to explore your offerings further. Visuals serve as a powerful tool to communicate the uniqueness and value of your store, setting you apart and fostering a strong connection with your audience.

Participate in Local and Community Events
For a computer store deeply rooted in the local community, participating in both virtual and in-person events holds immense value. These gatherings offer prime opportunities to connect with your target audience, network with fellow business owners, and engage directly with potential customers, creating meaningful interactions that go beyond traditional advertising.

By actively participating in local events, you position your computer store in the heart of the community, fostering relationships and strengthening your brand presence. Here's how these events can benefit your business:

Networking Opportunities: Events provide a platform to meet and collaborate with other local business owners, fostering partnerships that can mutually benefit each other's endeavors.

Direct Customer Interaction: Engaging with prospective customers face-to-face allows for personal connections. It's an ideal setting to showcase your products, share expertise, and address inquiries, thereby building trust and credibility.

Promotional Platform: Use these events as a promotional avenue to highlight special offers, exclusive deals, or upcoming products. Create a booth or display that captivates attendees and showcases the uniqueness of your computer store.

Community Integration: Participation in local events signifies your store's commitment to the community. It's an opportunity to support community initiatives, establish goodwill, and solidify your store's position as a valued local establishment.

Whether it's setting up a booth at a local fair, sponsoring a community event, or engaging in online forums, actively participating in local and community events aligns your computer store with the community's pulse. It's a chance to connect personally, forge meaningful relationships, and imprint your brand in the minds of local residents, ultimately contributing to long-term loyalty and success within your community.

Paid Advertising Strategies
If you're aiming to expand your computer store's reach rapidly, investing in paid advertising can be a game-changer. Here are some popular paid advertising methods to consider:

Television and Radio Ads: While a traditional approach, TV and radio ads offer extensive reach. They cover a broader audience but typically involve higher costs compared to other methods.

Promoted Social Media Posts: Transforming one of your store's social media posts into an ad allows for targeted promotion. You have the flexibility to select a specific audience, geographic region, and duration for running the ad. This method ensures your content reaches those most likely to engage with it.

Pay-Per-Click (PPC) Ads: This model charges you each time a user clicks on your ad. Platforms like Google offer PPC advertising, displaying your ad prominently at the top of search engine results for specific keywords you've chosen. It's a cost-effective way to target users actively searching for computer-related products or services.

Each of these paid advertising methods offers distinct advantages. Television and radio ads provide broad exposure, while promoted social media posts and PPC ads enable precise targeting, ensuring your message reaches the most relevant audience.

By strategically investing in paid advertising that aligns with your computer store's goals and target demographic, you can amplify visibility, drive traffic to your store, and generate valuable leads, ultimately contributing to the growth and success of your business.

Engage Your Audience with Workshops and Offers

As a computer store looking to make a mark, consider hosting workshops or webinars to share your expertise and solidify your position as a knowledgeable authority in your field. These sessions, whether online or in person, serve as invaluable platforms to impart specialized skills or technical know-how. By sharing valuable insights, you not only educate prospective customers but also establish meaningful connections within your industry. Additionally, these workshops present an opportunity to collect contact information from attendees, nurturing relationships for potential future business.

Another effective strategy is offering discounted or free products/services. Introductory discounts and complimentary trials act as enticing incentives for new customers, sparking their interest in your offerings. Encouraging referrals through customer-exclusive deals can amplify your customer base while fostering a sense of loyalty. Moreover, providing free samples or trials allows prospective customers to experience the quality of your products or services without a financial commitment. This approach builds trust and allows your offerings to speak for themselves, creating a strong foundation for future business relationships.

Remember, combining these strategies can amplify their impact. Investing in your business dreams is crucial, and a business banking expert can guide you on leveraging a business banking account to maximize your business's potential. By integrating these tactics, your computer store can elevate its visibility, foster trust with customers, and establish a solid foothold in the market, paving the way for sustained growth and success.

Chapter 9:
Operations and Logistics

Efficient operations and logistics are the backbone of a successful computer store. In this chapter, we will explore the intricacies of managing daily store operations, optimizing supply chain management, controlling inventory, and ensuring quality assurance to deliver a seamless shopping experience to your customers.

Daily Store Operations

Running a successful computer store involves a multitude of daily tasks and responsibilities that demand meticulous planning and execution. These operational processes are the backbone of the store's efficiency and customer satisfaction. Here's an overview of essential daily store operations:

Store Opening and Closing: Establishing clear opening and closing procedures is paramount to ensuring the seamless commencement and conclusion of each business day. These procedures encompass tasks such as securely unlocking and locking the premises, setting up enticing displays, and conducting closing inventory counts to maintain inventory accuracy.

Staff Scheduling: Crafting a well-structured daily staff schedule is critical for maintaining optimal staffing levels, especially during peak business hours. Efficient allocation of staff resources not only guarantees excellent customer service but also minimizes labor costs, contributing to overall operational effectiveness.

Customer Service: Prioritize customer service excellence by providing extensive training to your staff. This training should encompass welcoming and assisting customers, addressing their inquiries promptly, and ensuring a consistently pleasant shopping experience that fosters customer loyalty.

Checkout Process: Streamlining the checkout process is essential to minimize waiting times for customers. Implement efficient point-of-sale (POS) systems and provide comprehensive training to cashiers to facilitate swift and accurate transaction processing, enhancing customer satisfaction.

Store Maintenance: Regularly inspecting and maintaining the store's physical premises is crucial. This entails tasks such as routine cleaning, equipment maintenance, and promptly addressing any safety hazards to create a safe and pleasant shopping environment.

Merchandising: Ensuring that products are displayed attractively and that shelves remain well-stocked is pivotal in maximizing sales and customer engagement. Frequent restocking and strategic visual merchandising contribute to a dynamic and enticing shopping experience.

Order Fulfillment: If your store offers online and phone orders, it's imperative to efficiently manage order fulfillment. Timely processing and delivery or pickup of customer orders are essential for ensuring high levels of customer satisfaction and repeat business.

Security: Implementing comprehensive security measures, including surveillance cameras, alarms, and loss prevention strategies, is vital to protect against theft and to ensure the safety of both customers and employees. A secure shopping environment enhances customer trust.

Waste Management: Develop a robust waste management plan to effectively handle and dispose of both perishable and nonperishable items. This includes implementing recycling practices and adhering to environmental regulations, aligning your store with sustainable practices and responsible waste disposal.

The daily operations of a computer store are multifaceted and intricately interconnected. Effective management of these operations is pivotal in providing outstanding customer experiences, maintaining store efficiency, and ensuring the overall success of the business.

Supply Chain Management

Supply chain management plays a crucial role in the efficient and effective operation of a computer store. It involves the planning, coordination, and control of the flow of goods and information from suppliers to the store's shelves, with the ultimate goal of meeting customer demand while minimizing costs and maximizing profitability.

One of the key aspects of supply chain management for a computer store is vendor selection and management. Choosing reliable and cost-effective suppliers is essential to ensure a steady and high-quality supply of products. Computer stores often work with a variety of suppliers, including wholesalers, and distributors, to source products, packaged goods, and other items. Establishing strong relationships with these suppliers can lead to better pricing, timely deliveries, and access to unique products that can give the store a competitive edge.

Inventory management is another critical component of supply chain management for a computer store. Balancing inventory levels to meet customer demand while avoiding overstocking or understocking is a delicate task. Advanced inventory management systems and technologies can help store managers track product levels in real-time, forecast demand, and automatically reorder products when necessary. This reduces the risk of product spoilage, stockouts, and excess inventory, which can eat into profits.

Efficient transportation and logistics are vital for ensuring that products move smoothly from suppliers to the computer store's shelves. Computer stores often have multiple distribution centers to receive and distribute products to individual store locations. Optimizing routes, scheduling deliveries, and using technology like GPS tracking can help reduce transportation costs and ensure on-time deliveries. Moreover, eco-friendly transportation practices can align with sustainability goals and reduce the store's carbon footprint.

In today's highly competitive retail landscape, data analytics and technology play an increasingly significant role in supply chain management for computer stores. Collecting and analyzing data on customer preferences, sales trends, and inventory turnover can help stores make informed decisions about product assortment, pricing, and promotions. The use of RFID tags, barcodes, and advanced software systems can enhance inventory visibility, reduce errors, and streamline the replenishment process.

Effective supply chain management is essential for the success of a computer store. It involves vendor selection, inventory management, transportation, technology, data analytics, and compliance with safety regulations. By optimizing these aspects of the supply chain, computer stores can enhance customer satisfaction, reduce costs, and remain competitive in a dynamic and evolving retail industry.

Inventory Control

Inventory control is a crucial element of supply chain management that plays a pivotal role in various industries. It refers to the processes and strategies utilized by organizations to efficiently manage their stock of goods. Effective inventory control is essential for ensuring product availability, reducing carrying costs, avoiding stockouts, and optimizing overall business operations.

One of the primary objectives of inventory control is to find the right equilibrium between maintaining sufficient stock levels to meet customer demand and minimizing excess inventory. Excessive inventory can tie up valuable capital and storage space, increasing the risks of obsolescence and spoilage. Conversely, insufficient inventory can lead to stockouts, resulting in lost sales and customer dissatisfaction. Businesses employ inventory control methods to determine optimal stock levels for each product, relying on historical sales data, demand forecasts, and lead times.

Accurate and up-to-date record-keeping is fundamental to effective inventory control. This entails tracking the quantity, value, location, and movements of every item in the inventory. Modern businesses often utilize computerized inventory management systems that automate these tasks, offering real-time visibility into stock levels and facilitating rapid decision-making. These systems can generate reports on stock turnover rates, reorder points, and supplier performance, facilitating inventory control efforts.

The ABC analysis is a fundamental concept in inventory control, classifying products into categories based on their significance and value. "A" items represent high-value, high-priority products requiring meticulous monitoring and tighter control. "B" items hold moderate importance, while "C" items are low-value, low-priority products. This categorization enables businesses to allocate resources effectively, focusing efforts on managing the most critical items.

Inventory control strategies encompass various techniques for managing demand fluctuations and uncertainties. Safety stock, for instance, involves maintaining a buffer of extra inventory to account for unexpected demand surges or supply delays. Reorder points and economic order quantity (EOQ) calculations help determine when to reorder products to maintain desired stock levels while minimizing carrying costs. Just-in-time (JIT) inventory systems take an alternative approach, aiming to minimize inventory holding costs by receiving goods from suppliers precisely when needed.

Effective inventory control yields numerous benefits for businesses. It can reduce carrying costs associated with storage, insurance, and handling. It helps prevent overstocking, which ties up capital, and understocking, which results in missed sales opportunities. Furthermore, it contributes to stronger supplier relationships by providing accurate demand forecasts and ensuring timely replenishment orders.

Inventory control is an indispensable practice within supply chain management, aimed at striking a balance between optimal stock levels and minimal carrying costs. It involves the application of techniques such as ABC analysis, safety stock, EOQ, and JIT to streamline inventory management. By implementing effective inventory control strategies, businesses can enhance their overall efficiency, customer satisfaction, and financial performance.

Quality Assurance

Maintaining product quality is paramount in the computer business. Quality assurance measures help ensure that customers receive safe and fresh products:

Quality Standards: Establish and communicate clear quality standards for all products, including freshness, appearance, and packaging.

Vendor Compliance: Work closely with suppliers to ensure they adhere to quality and safety standards. Regularly audit and assess supplier practices.

Regular Inspections: Conduct routine inspections of products, checking for any signs of spoilage, damage, or expiration.

Employee Training: Train employees on proper handling and storage of products to maintain quality throughout the supply chain.

Recall Procedures: Develop clear procedures for handling product recalls. Communicate recalls to customers promptly and efficiently.

Efficient operations and logistics, coupled with a strong focus on quality assurance, are essential for the success and sustainability of your computer store. By carefully managing daily operations, optimizing your supply chain, controlling inventory, and ensuring product quality, you can provide a seamless shopping experience that keeps customers coming back.

Chapter 10:
Growth and Expansion

Expanding your computer store business is a significant step toward increasing profitability and market presence. In this chapter, we'll explore various strategies for growth and expansion, including broadening your product line, opening additional locations, considering franchising opportunities, and exploring international expansion.

Expanding Your Product Line

Diversifying your product offerings can breathe new life into your computer store and attract a broader customer base. Here's how to approach expanding your product line. begin with thorough market research to identify products in demand within your community. This step involves considering customer surveys, analyzing market trends, and assessing competitor offerings. By understanding what your customers want and what's currently popular, you can make informed decisions about which products to add to your inventory.

Strengthening your relationships with existing suppliers is crucial, and also seek out new ones to source the additional products you plan to offer. Building strong supplier partnerships ensures a consistent and reliable supply of new items, helping you maintain the quality and availability of your expanded product line.

As you expand your product line, it's essential to revise your inventory management strategies. This includes reevaluating your storage capacity, shelving layouts, and tracking systems. Adequate storage and efficient organization are key to managing a more diverse inventory effectively.

Your employees play a vital role in the success of your expanded product line. Ensure your staff is knowledgeable about the new products and can assist customers with inquiries. Consider providing specialized training where necessary to enhance their expertise and confidence when dealing with the new offerings.

Creating effective marketing campaigns is crucial to introducing the new products to your customer base. Utilize a mix of strategies, including in-store displays, digital advertising, and promotional events, to generate interest and inform your customers about the exciting additions to your inventory.

Once the new products are on the shelves, continuously gather customer feedback. This valuable input allows you to fine-tune your offerings and make adjustments based on customer preferences. Listening to your customers and responding to their needs helps ensure the long-term success of your expanded product line.

Expanding your product line can be a strategic move to grow your computer store business. However, it should be approached systematically, with careful consideration of market research, supplier relationships, inventory management, employee training, marketing efforts, and ongoing customer feedback. By following these steps, you can effectively diversify your product offerings and attract a wider customer base while maintaining customer satisfaction and profitability.

Opening Additional Locations

Expanding your computer store by opening additional locations can significantly increase your reach and market share. However, this endeavor involves a series of crucial considerations to ensure a successful expansion.

Location Selection: One of the most critical factors in opening new computer store locations is selecting the right spot. Conduct thorough location analysis to identify areas with high foot traffic, underserved markets, or demographics that align with your target customer base. Understanding the local market dynamics and competition is essential in making an informed decision.

Legal and Regulatory Requirements: Before proceeding with a new location, it's vital to navigate the legal and regulatory landscape. Ensure you understand and comply with local zoning laws, permits, and regulations specific to the computer retail industry. Failing to do so can lead to costly delays and complications.

Financial Planning: Create a comprehensive financial plan for the new location. This plan should include detailed projections of startup costs, operating expenses, and revenue expectations. Securing the necessary financing or capital to fund the expansion is essential to ensure a smooth launch and sustained growth.

Staffing: The success of a new store often hinges on the quality and readiness of your staff. Begin the hiring and training process well in advance of the opening to ensure that the team is adequately prepared to serve customers and manage operations. Consistency in service quality across all locations is key to maintaining your brand's reputation.

Supply Chain Management: Expanding to additional locations requires a reevaluation of your supply chain and logistics operations. Consider centralizing warehousing and distribution to ensure consistent product availability across all stores. Efficient supply chain management is crucial for minimizing costs and ensuring product freshness.

Marketing and Branding: Developing a solid marketing strategy is essential to introduce the new location to the community. Leverage your existing brand identity, but be prepared to customize it to the local market. Tailoring your marketing efforts to reflect the unique characteristics and preferences of the new location can help build a loyal customer base.

Monitoring and Evaluation: After opening, continuously monitor the performance of the new location. Establish key performance indicators (KPIs) to assess its success and compare it to your initial projections. Be prepared to make adjustments to operations, marketing, and staffing based on the data and feedback received to ensure the ongoing success of the new store.

In conclusion, opening additional locations for your computer store can be a rewarding strategy for growth, but it requires careful planning and execution. By addressing location selection, legal requirements, financial planning, staffing, supply chain management, marketing, and ongoing evaluation, you can increase your chances of a successful expansion and enhance your market presence.

Franchising Opportunities

Franchising opportunities offer a unique avenue for business expansion and growth. This business model allows entrepreneurs to replicate a successful and established brand, concept, or product by licensing the rights to operate under the parent company's name and guidance. Here, we delve into the key aspects of franchising opportunities.

One of the primary advantages of franchising is the ability to tap into a proven business model. Franchisors typically have a track record of success, a well-developed business plan, and a strong brand identity. This can reduce the risks associated with starting a new business from scratch and increase the likelihood of profitability.

For entrepreneurs, franchising offers a level of independence while still benefiting from the support and resources of an established brand. Franchisees can leverage the franchisor's expertise in areas such as marketing, operations, and supply chain management. This support can be especially beneficial for individuals who may have limited experience in running a business.

Franchising opportunities also come with a ready-made customer base. Established brands often have a loyal following, which can translate into a steady stream of customers from day one. This can significantly reduce the time and effort required to build brand recognition and attract customers.

However, it's crucial for potential franchisees to carefully evaluate the terms and conditions of the franchise agreement. Franchise agreements outline the responsibilities and obligations of both the franchisor and the franchisee. These agreements often include details about fees, royalties, territorial restrictions, and operational standards. Prospective franchisees should seek legal and financial advice to ensure they fully understand the terms before committing.

Franchising opportunities extend to various industries, from fast food and retail to fitness centers and service businesses. The choice of franchise should align with the interests, skills, and financial capacity of the potential franchisee. Conducting thorough market research and due diligence is essential to select the right franchise that matches one's goals and resources.

Once a franchise is established, ongoing communication and collaboration between the franchisor and franchisee are critical.

Franchisees benefit from regular training, updates on best practices, and support in addressing operational challenges. Franchisors, in turn, rely on franchisees to maintain the brand's reputation and uphold quality standards.

In conclusion, franchising opportunities provide a pathway for entrepreneurs to enter the business world with the backing of an established brand and support structure. It offers a balance between independence and guidance, making it an appealing option for those looking to start their own businesses. However, due diligence and a clear understanding of the franchise agreement are essential to ensure a successful and mutually beneficial partnership between franchisor and franchisee.

Each of these growth and expansion strategies comes with its own set of opportunities and challenges. The choice of which path to pursue should align with your business goals, resources, and risk tolerance. Careful planning, market research, and a commitment to maintaining the quality and values of your computer store are essential elements of successful growth and expansion in the highly competitive computer industry.

Conclusion

Starting and running a successful computer store is a challenging but rewarding endeavor. In this comprehensive guide, we have explored every facet of this journey, from the initial considerations of why to start a computer store and whether it's the right fit for you, to the intricate details of market research, legal considerations, financing, store design, staffing, marketing, operations, and various expansion strategies.

The computer store industry is a dynamic and competitive one, marked by changing consumer preferences, evolving technologies, and shifting market trends. To thrive in this environment, you must be adaptable, customer-focused, and committed to delivering a top-notch shopping experience.

Key takeaways from this guide include:

Understanding Your Market: Thorough market research is the foundation of your computer store's success. Knowing your target audience, competition, and location dynamics will guide your business decisions.

Legal and Regulatory Compliance: Navigating the legal and regulatory landscape is crucial. Choosing the right business structure, obtaining permits, and ensuring health and safety compliance are non-negotiable steps.

Financing and Budgeting: Carefully estimate your startup costs, secure funding, and manage your finances diligently. Budgeting and financial planning are essential for long-term sustainability.

Store Design and Layout: A well-designed store layout, effective shelving, and attractive merchandising contribute to a pleasant shopping experience that keeps customers coming back.

Product Selection and Suppliers: Building strong relationships with suppliers, managing inventory efficiently, setting competitive prices, and exploring private label options are key to product selection and procurement.

Staffing and Management: Hiring and training a motivated team, establishing employee policies, efficient scheduling, and performance evaluation are essential for smooth store operations.

Marketing and Promotion: Developing a comprehensive marketing plan, building a strong brand image, implementing effective advertising strategies, and utilizing loyalty programs are vital for attracting and retaining customers.

Operations and Logistics: Managing daily store operations, optimizing supply chain management, controlling inventory, and maintaining quality assurance are the cornerstones of a well-run computer store.

Growth and Expansion: Strategies such as expanding your product line, opening additional locations, exploring franchising opportunities, and venturing into international markets offer avenues for growth and expansion.

In the computer store business, customer satisfaction is paramount. By providing a wide variety of quality products, exceptional service, and a seamless shopping experience, you can build a loyal customer base and position your store for long-term success.

Remember that success in the computer industry requires ongoing adaptability, a commitment to innovation, and a dedication to maintaining the highest standards of quality and customer service. As you embark on this journey, may this guide serve as a valuable resource to help you navigate the challenges and seize the opportunities that come your way in the world of computer retail. Best of luck on your path to building a thriving computer store business.

www.ingramcontent.com/pod-product-compliance
Lightning Source LLC
Chambersburg PA
CBHW062350290526
45794CB00005B/2168